Invisible Foreground traces a journey from childhood into an adult
world that is filled with tenderness, terror, and the wish for secure
familial surroundings. Always on the verge of disappearing into
a fractured memory the speaker is both sure and unsure of, these
poems embroider lived reality with dreams of the imagination.
Suburban houses, provincial terrain, furniture, feelings, physical
desire (among other things) all serve, in the mind of the poet, as
emotional set designs for a half century of life as performance.

I am blighted by home decor

Invisible Foreground

David Bateman

Frontenac House
Calgary, Alberta

Book and cover design: Epix Design
Author photo: Serafin

Library and Archives Canada Cataloguing in Publication

Bateman, David
         Invisible foreground / David Bateman.

Poems.
ISBN 1-897181-78-7

         I. Title.

PS8553.A8254I68 2005   C811'.54   C2005-900346-4

We acknowledge the support of the Canada Council for the Arts which last year invested $20.3 million in writing and publishing throughout Canada. We also acknowledge the support of The Alberta Foundation for the Arts.

**Canada Council
for the Arts**

**Conseil des Arts
du Canada**

Printed and bound in Canada
Published by Frontenac House Ltd.
1138 Frontenac Avenue S.W. Calgary, Alberta, T2T 1B6, Canada
Tel: 403-245-2491   Fax: 403-245-2380
editor@frontenachouse.com   www.frontenachouse.com

1 2 3 4 5 6 7 8 9 09 08 07 06 05

For Amy

Acknowledgements

Some of the poems in this collection have appeared in the following publications: *The Peterborough Review; Prairie Fire, Race Poetry eh?; Dandelion; Filling Station; Terrain, finewords chapbooks; There is Something Terrible about a Collection of Guitars, Peterborough Poets, wordworks.*

A special thank you to Rose Scollard for coming to a reading at Prairie Ink in Calgary one night and making me feel like Lana Turner being discovered at Schwabb's Drugstore. To everyone at Frontenac House Press, and to a community of poets across Canada who I feel honoured to know and to work among. The list is endless – to name a few:

bill bissett, Derek Beaulieu, Emily Cargan, Jason Christie, Beth Core, Jeramy Dodds, Cameron Esler, Charnie Guettel, Jill Hartman, Larissa Lai, Nicole Markotic, Ashok Mathur, Stephen McDonald, Tom Muir, Rajinderpal S. Pal, Cathy Petch, Sharron Proulx, Nikki Reimer, Sharanpal Ruprai, R.M.Vaughan, Fred Wah, Jonathon C. Wilcke, Sheri-D Wilson, and Rita Wong.

Contents

Invisible Foreground

Storey-and-a-half

the end of the second world war signalled
the beginning of a new kind of man
we all know this
one of them was my father
he walked directly out of the trenches with his stories of
Normandy
entangled with the stories he had been told by other soldiers
my grandfather's version of Vimy Ridge
a geographic location
linguistically suited to drunken war stories

(by way of an offensive xenophobic trope
Vimy sounds like a mispronunciation of a word that doesn't exist)

my father came
stories in tow
directly from those traumatized sites
into our living room
in a house he built
on a marshy plot of land that shifted sank and cracked
the foundations of every storey-and-a-half
he had built his life upon

he struggled for years
in car lots, real estate agencies, and on construction sites
until finally he drove off the side of the road
Vimy slurring in his memory
his children
tumbling like dice inside a small car
he did not survive
the land was traumatized
and when well meaning war veterans groups
developed the Veterans Land Act
my father borrowed a substantial sum of money
in order to improve his home, brick front storey-and-a-half
we bought green shag carpet, linoleum, a new refrigerator
I was obsessed with raking the carpet on the stairs

and in the living room
and when daddy fell from scaffolding on a construction site
he had to spend a year in a rented hospital bed
in the middle of our parlour
in a sea of well groomed shag carpet
in a body cast that covered his entire torso
raised his shattered shoulder
elegant humourless plaster ball gown
with part of a broom handle planted in hard white matter

and when the doctor removed the bodice
and pulled his arm down
twelve months later, he fainted, fell down
retreated back into trenches of emasculated discourse

and I had begun to identify myself with the land
with the myth and truth of Vimy and Normandy
and our living room carpet
my prairie and my mountain my hospital bed
my sea and my river the comfort of claustrophobic hills
and dales overforested by God
and so many attractive well meaning environmentalists
my father's body as desired land

I lost my mind in these tyrannous locations
there was a white leatherette rocker
furniture was like countries to me then

in the far northeast corner of our living room
father would sit and drink
and in a dream I imagine a rifle in his arms
directed at me and I ask him not to
and the dream ends
and many years later I travelled by bus
through the Negev desert to Eilat and the Red Sea
exhausted I slept and reiterated that dream
but at the end daddy lifts his rifle and it becomes a guitar
and we move from one imaginary site
to the grassy hills of another

and my friends are dancing and singing
and I wake to know my dream
could only happen once my father had died

and I seek answers from the fragments of my psyche
that remember this imaginary time
when my dad was gone and then he returns
and I cannot seem to identify places
but there are specific war memorial parks cenotaphs
Pre-Raphaelite sculptures of God and
dark cast athletic men beckoning to each other this
armistice of love I feel for my father

but my dad was never gone
I know that
but I remember his absence in some imagined terrain
so distinctly and I know that it is there
and that it did not exist in real time and space
it was desirous and always on the horizon
but I could never reach it as I was raised where

tree lines interfere with horizons
when I go to land that asserts itself disallows intervention
I am distant, awed and somewhat relieved
by the claustrophobic grammar of my prison sentence
by puns
by no real felt obligation to make sense of any of this
save the scars on my ideas of order, of the world,
so profoundly destabilized

environmentalists frighten me
so I invent new ways of fearing
for every room every landscape
nonchalant confident and a little skittish
I quickly grow bored with my own terror
and redecorate the terrain of every site I visit
blighted by home décor
I do not want to save the land I want it to save me

in small rooms, broadloom and a modest acorn hearth
it was the second world war slipping into the seventies
and the shift in masculine identity and shag carpet
the recuperative rights of war veterans and their teenaged sons
these gendered hegemonic spectacles that take me into meadows
and my uncle's hands become the hands of my first lover
the only beautiful man I could ever re-invent over and over again
stories in halves duplicated by memory and time

meadows and sunlight that evaporate inhibition
this obsessive raking over memories and hearts

I cannot self-identify with landscape
raised in dales by brooks
and the soft incestuous hands of buttercups
and Queen Anne's lace made to dance in blackface
in the snow in stifling sunlight where the reductive
reflective shallow gaze of creeks and murky rivers
and all those interminable Ontario maples
the birch my father loved

I love and resist the prairie poet and I do not dwell
in mountains or on beaches
I pose on beaches
and my sites my points of reference
close me in and scatter all my land

mesmerized by the site of my own blood
I take terrain inside and rake and rake and rake
because the forest and the trees
the glamourous light
confuse me and make me want to cower
in a glade by a plane
enclosures vast unwalled I resist
and contradict the language of my land

Elvis (excerpted from *Jackie O: The Show She Never Gave*)

I have been party to Elvis sightings on squalid sun scorched spring break infested beaches in southern Florida where pock marked Vegas styled zircon encrusted deejays ran with cordless mikes through swarms of bikini clad locusts and sang ozone bursting renditions of *Burning Love*.

I have seen his king sized bed in the Elvis museum in a strip mall in Orlando where my dear mother looked at me at the checkout as I made my purchase of *Love Me Tender* conditioner and shampoo and she said to me, in all seriousness, "Poor Elvis. I wonder what was botherin' him?"

Not sightings of the ethereal kind, not the dead Elvis resurrected within an endless deep fried crucifixion of Burger Kings, laundromats and donut shops.

Not sightings as proof that he never really died. Rather, sightings of the very earthly and tangible kind.

Icons are made to endure a hundred marketable seasons or more glaucoma, hypertension, an enlarged heart, clogged arteries, a twisted colon, enormous doses of uppers and downers, a crucifix, a Star of David & an Ankh around his neck, taking care of business, no need to offend heaven on a technicality.

But even near death he had a remarkable head of hair.

Stark insane voice on some liminal horizon

hawk moon nights misspell imitative
as cowboys find disproportionate surprise
among high heeled leather boots
lipstick brands on cowhide
and the faint masculine gaze
of their forefathers

It was never Lana Turner
It was always me

sleeping with husbands demands
a particular nostalgia for someone else's
present

Hitler's intervention kept Esther Williams
from the Olympics
doomed to cinematic glory and aquacades
she developed no capacity to embrace
cross-dressed lovers

long line bathing suits as cages for
vast tracts of flesh and land
are always situated
on the horizon of desire
polka dot bikinis are islands
that are easy to get to
by delicate boat-like footsteps

Clumsy presidents with sons the size
of the Saskatchewan River
deface this rocky stare
John Wilkes Booth was a tragic actor

for years Cher believed that Mount Rushmore
was a natural phenomenon
I believe in Cher

clothing is a verb
as raglan-sleeved cowl-necked
jumpers race and interfere
with majestic hysteria

bumper stickers cry out
"I date your husband"

inflected grief like the
stain of a very ripe peach

that part of "Imitation of Life" where Laura
throws herself on her mother's coffin
and takes all the blame for John
Gavin's whiteness
never fails to reduce me to a
particular kind of over-educated
undernourished weeping
early twenty-first century faggot
who misidentifies with Lana Turner's glamour
and the poems of Emily Dickinson
sung to the tune of
"The Yellow Rose of Texas"

in the nineteen sixties I was much younger
than I wanted to be
named my first cat after a thin fashion model
went to a masquerade as Twiggy
and was asked why I didn't wear a costume
eyeliner like vertical tears inscribes
itself upon my expectant glare

and when the past comes back to haunt you
where does it come back from?

Samuel Goldwyn was no match for
a tall faintly masculine female swimmer
who would go on to love all the wrong men in briefs
and uniforms of over-evolved masculinity

butterfly strokes disable small winged creatures
slur their speech
flying into opaque surfaces
on the horizon of desire
they are easier to reach than the translucent glass
of a reflective present

Pale green is the colour of my love
standing in for emotion
blue, blue
watered down haikus
soup, light
an impressionist painting
and some forms of courage

I dress myself in adjectives
that describe the way I feel about everything
absence weaving shawls of
delightful degradation

Emily

I saw the face of Jesus in my crumpled gold Ikea bath towel
on the floor of the second storey bathroom

we placed the aquarium beneath the Emily Carr
on the west wall
it was one of those freestyle Cezanne-esque pieces
done on cardboard

"did she do it with her fingers?"

a glorious affront to Emily, Jesus
and overproduced Swedish furniture
the afterbirth of originality renders everything a copy
and our homes become comfortable unsuitable self-made
cathedrals
for the outward expression of our souls

"that tenuous relief that holds a Cezanne together"

only makes sense to me
when I see it in your eyes
and fall apart
and swim there in pieces in small glass
enclosed pools just under heaven
and the billowing middle class totemic sentiments
that keep my faith intact

I get a little weepy

I get a little weepy waiting for the #1 Bowness bus
and I know there were no ideas of order in Key West last spring
only hot tubs, off season rates, misreading modernist poems
leaving midnite pickups at 3 a.m.
when he threatens to rent roller blades that afternoon

if I ever buy roller blades
fly me to the Encantadas
and shoot me there

and besides, he was from Cleveland
where there is no end to line dancing
shell art, mid-western couples
who still read Playboy
Jeffrey Dahmer was the boy next door
"Interesting Asia" was never very far away
boys who won't become men
make very good wives
apologize, please, for all the misplaced verbs, lives

so I'm illiterate, sue me
sharing stories on this midnite bus
I transfer to hell in handcarts
pre-designed by urban planners
who not only trace the colour of skin
the slant of wrist, feathers, strollers, caps
the demographics of a well turned phrase

they know who we are
they saw what we did

Joan Crawford's shoulder pads mean more to us
than making sense of this pale art
Hell's Angels make our neighbourhood
– how can I say? –
inhabitable

what I meant was
I am superficial and I get a little weepy
waiting for the #1 Bowness bus

come Hell's Angels or high water
I'll be in the Keys late May
weather's beautiful
wish you were

Terrain

A few days before my thirty-eighth birthday
I drove downstate
from Ontario
through the Adirondacks
and back again

Mother slept all the way
I would watch the rise and fall
of the small delicate hairs on her chin
they would have to go
before we got to the visitation

Somewhere near Vineland
the fruit stands closed for fall
tears began to store themselves
in deep recesses of memory
above my cheeks

I was destined, deranged,
determined not to let them out
clutched the soft flat
impression of thin cardboard
in my breast pocket

I wore funeral drag
a cheap linen shirt
black full pleated trousers a bad cotton blend
black leather hand-me-down shoes
with the tassels cut off

tassels annoy me

By the time we reached the Falls
the storage of grief
was at such a point of lunacy
Teresa Stratas was singing Kurt Weill
"Buddy on the Night Shift"

I bypassed the Falls
they are so beautiful
like the delicate rise and fall
of those light hairs
like mist on an old escarpment

I compare her to the land

We arrived an hour early
I remembered the off ramps and the landmarks
the bronze David on a knoll
at the exit to Elmwood Avenue
all the streets and the drive-thrus
it all came back without courtesy, with contempt

Mother woke up at Customs for a moment
mumbled citizenship, a perfect potential smuggler
so sweet, so silent, so sly
lingering in sleep until we reached the suburbs
there were no Adirondacks

I just wanted there to be mountains
not that flat interminable Ontario highway
above the escarpment and over the river
upstate New York, downstate Ontario
wanting to drive through pleasing imaginary terrain

instead of places we are destined for

would trade for high
inviolable peaks
these raw impressions
random
scars

In the mall near the funeral home
we bought a sympathy card and flowers
nail polish and cigarettes
disposable razors
I trimmed those long delicate
hairs that were suddenly grey and coarse
no longer mist

in a parking lot in another light

Her nails were so dirty
the rose polish was on her skirt
I was angry for all the wrong reasons
refused to go to her sister's house
the widow, not that

Seeing the places where we lay together
all those lies, gasps, moans
sweet, silent, sly
bent over pool tables
beside work benches

walking through those little rooms
I would only clutch and tear
the soft flat cardboard impression
in my breast pocket
saving me

I swept the heat from my forehead
we drove by that grocery store I remembered
where I met his two friends from Fort Erie
who fed me Campari and tied me up
in weak knots
I laughed at their adventure

Finally parked with all the family cars
by the big stone parlour,
like a large suburban home
imperfect, glistening, strange

In we went
ahead of everyone
her breath was so bad
I had planned it to be so perfect
to bathe her and prepare some false scene

I failed, tired early
bought her new clothes in a cheap department store
and became so afraid of the whole idea
panicky by midnight the night before
called at seven a.m. to cancel

she was so disappointed

We went, people came to us
relatives from Ontario sat with us
we talked, wept a little
there were two services
both to be dull in

One at the funeral home
one at the church
the church was beautiful
the singing nasal, small imperfect vacuum cleaner of a voice
I longed for Patsy Cline, a perfect eulogy

"You Belong To Me"

The widow looked like Ethel Kennedy
wore tight cheap white satin, a very bad fit
we knew him in the same way
we shared his lust, wanting, unwillingly
everyone knew

The service was long
I ate the body of Christ, lean, frail, whitened lies
thought it would serve his memory
I was awkward and didn't know what to do
he had to slip it into my mouth

God gave me a strained flirtatious look as I walked away

The food was very good
the aboveground pool and the well stocked outdoor fridge
the mini-bar and the chaise
all that furniture and carpet
and all those major appliances
the talk of private schools

We left mid-afternoon
drove back by Lewiston
a shorter route
she slept again, soft, shaven
the smooth flat roads through peaceful territory, lined, tolled

On the way into the city
on the expressway
I pulled the slim card from my breast pocket
intimations of his breath from beside soft flat cardboard
saving me

the serenity prayer on his prayer card

He had no idea
my abuser
I loved his face
and his body
his Christ-like devotion

His mild inept directives, loose knots
his gentle touch
a brutal satiate way
of hiding
into death

I walked to the theatre around seven forty-five
mother was safe back at the retirement home
I could have taken her
but it had to be my night alone in the seventh row

the night before my thirty-eighth birthday

this strained flirtatious date with myself

She was incredible, god-like
at seventy
moving with such slow deliberate self assurance
this icon
this misty geographic form

These two events together
this deliberate
destined date with myself
awkward, rhymed
alone

He's gone
there was no grace in his fall
his luck surpassed our grief
he was cared for into dying
golfed only days before he died

Flew home early from the daughter's in Florida
the daughter who tries so hard to hate me
died at home, in Buffalo
the Queen City
named after me

He had asked the Priest why he had cancer
received some apocryphal non-answer
when his life
would
suffice

only soft, flat cardboard saves me, gilded, lined, embossed

A ticket
to a good show, a revival
gay times good friends

no memories
cheap wine

She sang
"So Long Dearie"
"Put On Your Sunday Clothes"
with all the grace and self-assurance
I somehow miss

I cried more watching Carol Channing
on the opening night of a world tour of
Hello Dolly
than I did at his funeral
the soft flat card of theatre tickets comforts me
Broadway comforts me, a passport photo of him as a teenager
comforts me

Uneasy with this comfort strangers ask
who the attractive man is on the bulletin board
across from my bed
one of my alcoholics, my abuser, beloved
I take long journeys to forget him

endless semiological road trips through mountains, rivers
imaginary cultural terrain
there are no melodies, show tunes, a dirge
there are ways of seeing
all of this through mist

The love I have for the places, people
the locations of all my pain, cities
to go in and out of spaces, caves
and find his face so close
to mine

along some old escarpment, mist

imagined, real
terrain

Watching grown men cry

1

over cappuccino with a warm shot of whiskey beside a thin young woman on a barstool in a lounge named "East of Never" under pressure in a late night board meeting when his son will be the eastern star by nine in a first grade play named "Heaven" after stand-up sex with his golfing buddy in a fully equipped RV while the wives are at the spa when the flirtatious lesbian economy of the straight women he works under excludes and excites him before undressing for dinner in full frontal perusal of twenty-five years of living he will never get back beside the pane-fused light of a sun razed moon on a surreal jigsaw on a commode in his den regardless of pomegranate salad sun dried children sent to camp she asks him to go down on her again with his shallow feet awakening in a sudden stream of light and some fragility in shadows

2

inside a posh holding bin for new psychiatric patients interrogating $2000 red leather Barcelona knock-offs below a wreath of holiday wealth imagining belief in small paternalistic doses without regard for nothing less than fine wine praise for middle aged women sunglasses and scarves beyond question the faint vivacious tremor of her lower lips inside identity defined by birth certificates driver's licences genital configurations and undotted sin above reproach for moody playoff seasons male menopausal breath beneath cribbage boards plastic pegs hedge clippings and the news of the world unless heaven allows foundational bliss and flood insurance

Slight Xmas

My flying anorexic Santa
in red baggy bone racked satin
black brass buckled
platform boots

Pubic pearls for tears
tawny fishnet sack
small gifts
sentimentalized reindeer

Rudolph weeping at the helm
a phobia for dark narrow shafts
kissing mommy, fire underfoot
late night world tours

Free yourself from stockings
run barefoot on another beach
braid your beard
take the Christ back out of

an excuse to shop

Semi-detached

the appalling majesty of the suburbs
communes of fortune
legacy of evolving house husbands/wives
men's eyes
circular stares
cases of imported beer
me and my fifty
brew, toil, trouble

corporate logos
on the furniture

at home here Helen, Troy
in this never ending story
of greed, ginger, rye

to crave the present of nostalgia here
in these quaint tombs
queer treed lots
semis, singles
backyards like holding pens for propane
pessimism, pork cutlets
and a never ending taste for cheap zinfandel

the spare and fragile strength of Jumbo Shrimp
of sand and snow
poplars, birch, group homes
foundling maples into infant evergreens

hot tubs, the sound of trains beyond the fortress wall
intimating life outside this camp atrocious kitsch
this glorious denial

I want to live
here!

Homage to your latest hair transplant

I will send you a weeping telegram
and cry all over that faux marbleized shelf
you sent me from the ivory coast

Stella

He lived on a Point on the edge of America
and when he made love to me,
it was like a small white cloud descending on my face.

Soft deep and wet, his kisses extended far beyond
the limited parameters of my narrow but bountiful smile.

He would use the uppermost regions of my thighs as
a vagina of sorts. By lubricating sparingly
we were able to create, with the
aid of his national endowment,
an extremely pleasurable little mechanism.

Like the popular song of its day,
he made me feel like a natural woman.

We spent the last two days of 1996 together.
The first year of the second half of the final decade
of the twentieth century
ended for me, in his arms.

He took a long time to ejaculate,
up to fifteen minutes of soft sinewy pumping
in and out of my makeshift cunt.
After 30 to 45 minutes of tender passionate
foreplay, the large head of his penis
against my thighs and rubbing just
below my testicles, he renewed my faith
in the endless lifelong possibilities
for new sexual adventure.

It wasn't a radically new act.
It just worked so well with him.
He was a perfect lover in many ways.
About to reach orgasm,
he would always whisper, "Oh baby."
That made me feel brand new.
Worn out but brand new.

On the morning of New Year's Day, as I massaged his back,
he said to me, in his faint beautiful southern accent, "God bless
you."

I loved him a little. He seemed kind and decent
and he was very easy to be around.
When we showered together he would wash me everywhere,
from head to toe.

He was a sculptor, a situationalist, had models for an
environmental shrine on an endless river.
Everything with him was so stark, so
uncomplicated. But that was my fleeting impression.
I knew him for a very short time.

The week before I arrived he had taken in a stray dog,
beautiful luminescent coat covering dry flaking putrescent skin.
He found her on a visit to the French Quarter, bundled her up
glamourous urban migrants on an uneasy pilgrimage of love
called himself "a courtesan caught in the headlights"
I loved the dooms of his greying nonchalance.

Through the night as we made love, and slept,
I could hear her cough and
gag in the back room of his flat.

He named her Kee Soo Mahn, he said it was Sanskrit for flower.
Kind strangers would pet her, ask her
name, and after having it explained to them, would use the
English translation.

He changed her name to Stella

Perhaps it seemed harmless to them to neglect the ethnic details
of a dog's life.

Decided to re-name her Stella so that he
could call her when she was lost in the Quarter

and it would sound like that beautiful flatulent howl
that almost begins one of the saddest plays
of the twentieth century.

He spoke to her when she was still Flower,
English for Kee Soo Mahn,
her shit rust coat shimmering in the winter sun,
as we sat in an outdoor cafe drinking Darjeeling tea.
He said to her, "you have given up your freedom
for a longer life."

He fed her antibiotics every morning
and would make a special trip near dusk, on the ferry, to walk her.
I was glad to relinquish my very fettered freedom,
stranded in the fog, for a few short days with him and his dog on
that Point in America

Slow, soft, and easy.
We made love like there would be many tomorrows.
Some of them we would spend together.
But to spend all of them with one person was something that I
would never come to expect of myself or of Matthew,
or of anyone else on God's green earth.

He was just another special person
I would take with me in photographs and memories,
and line my soul with the thought of him,
and his slow wet tantalizing way of going down on me.

His thick dark chest hair was like a welcome mat to my face.
I made my lips an open invitation to his full soft buttocks
covered in light fair hair.

His head was round and kind and peaceful and mostly covered in
light brown straight hair.

The hair on a person's body hypnotizes me. I watch
strands, even the smallest ones, lying still.
I always long to see them, even the smallest ones, move.

The movement of hair on a lover's body represents
for me the end of an affair.

The hair on his body never seemed to move.

I had such a sad expectant longing to see that happen.
So with him the longing never ended.

It just went on and on and on. It could go on forever.
But so long as it didn't move, I was safe. Surprised.

I would watch him on the ferry, and even the lightest wind would
tease me in its promise to move his hair for me.
It just seemed to stay still
frozen in romance, at bay.

It must have been moving in some small way.
Especially on the stronger windier southern days
by an aging river threatening to swallow itself
in urban transfer. But I never saw it moving, the wind,
his body hair.

There was such slow temptation in my eyes for him.
I was on reserve.
Motion was not something I could let inside my heart then.
So it all stood still.

I have only vague memories of the hair in his nose.
It could not have had much of an impression on me
or I would have remembered it in great detail.

His pubic hair, like his chest hair, was welcoming, warm,
a supple place for my smile to rest upon.

Just below the circumcised head of his penis I remember
a dry rough part, a ring, a cap.
It made me curious, but not enough to ask.

I made myself the mute explorer, all the time wondering what
these regions were, and what they meant, but only tasting,
touching, and moving right along.

I was no Christopher Columbus.
There were no claims to be made,
no native habit to be intruded upon, nothing flat made round.
Just a happy wanderer, a nomad of sorts. A sly transient slut with
no reward but the smile on my face and the way in which I tattoo
each place I have been on his body on my heart.

The way in which my mind photographs each patch of hair, and
makes it still.

These are positive images I build in my fortieth year.
Attempting love in all the right places, all the same places I have
always been. Instead of longing, in maturity, for this equals sign,
this sum, this end of an equation.

I want no mathematics of love from him, and I teach myself with
each new lover not to expect as much.

The quality of love for some of us is strained by
necessary safety and too much needless longing
for some one and only.

I have him.
on the edge of America
and on the hairs on the back of my neck,
and the ones I seldom shave on my big toes, and the ones
I remove with cream for strapless gowns
that shimmer and rustle in the river wind
between goose bumps on the backs of my arms.
My father's stubble at the top of my forehead,
and the small frail harvest hairs lining the insides of my ears.
I obsess upon these things, these transient mutable reminders of
the mortality of love and how it exceeds in every way the
weakness we may feel in other parts of our everyday lives.

Matthew had a friend who told him that Tennessee Williams
once lived across the courtyard from him, and when Tennessee
brought young men home Matthew's friend could hear him
calling out, one assumes during great moments of intimacy,
"My little pony, my little pony."

Comical and beautiful. I imagine the hairs at the base of the neck
of all those beautiful boys, those ponies, and all the warm winter
wind that will pass between my lips, and the lips of strangers I
will meet
over and over and over again. Like harvest,
like fog, like river wind, like kindness.
Like all of the plays all of the time.

Like no end to a romance I never saw coming, but hit head on.
I am this fearless driver...

Local colour (fabulous pastoral lament)

dandelions seeding
buttercups in full bloom
fireflies dance the tarantella
fields blue with blankets
green marked by deceptive old earth
tones of barns that claim to remedy the land

there are no remedies
only quiet slowing lives re-make the earth
I re-make land as I cross it in distracting array
brushing up against the dirt
saving remedy for contrast, filth
I disembowel this posing
this original

colourless fakes
riotous ritualistic beige procreative lies
bland determinist industrial mystique
I see this crass translucent heterosexual dream diminishing
in squalid evening light

as soft as
buttercups, blankets, fields
flies, Crisco, dandelions

blue
these blankets
green deceptive raiment

there is shelter in stoles, pearls
handbags born from old deceptive earth
tones

re-dress my silent growing country rage
heels raised tractors ready set toes girls go!

Calgary airport

I like to go to the airport
check into Swiss Chalet
order a baked potato
and one of those tiny bottles of bad
white Chardonnay

gaze across the avenue
at Riley & McCormick's Western Wear Boutique
covet hatboxes, beaded belts, sleek brass eagle buckles
watch the simulacric cowboys come and go
as they conjure dreams of Patsy and Hank Snow

I like to change my money into lire, drachmas,
pesos, yen (and back again)
pull out my battered cordless laptop
play video games at the bar by the gate
and wonder who came first
the chicken or the hen

write some cowboy doggerel
throw back a bloody Caesar a pitcher of Long Island Iced Tea
inventing espadrilles, piñatas, cocktails
suede handbags, husbands, well behaved children
a new level of five star intimacy by the sea

gaze longingly at the inflatable bottles
of imported Mexican beer
bite passionately into the slice of lime lounging
at the bottom of my empty Caesar
buy a bolo tie
imagine the world queer

take a taxi home
to my fictional unemployed boyfriend
the sloe death fizz
of my cheap gin romance
a pigfoot and a bottle of beer

Edna (for Charnie)

I pack my Auden
with Canadian Tire money
mark the pages
where my heart has been

I will be nothing when I am a corpse
but will have lived in trailer parks, beaver meads
when meadows became ashtrays
and the red and gold of the F.W. Woolworth sign
seemed the only beautiful thing left in the world

So many places accept Canadian Tire money
so many hearts have been broken
mine remains, what remains, Edna
of this delicate shindig, this hullabaloo
are fervent moistened pages
you

Breath

Love's not special
Love's just breathing in and out

Tears aren't special
Tears are just the excrement of doubt

I'm not special
I'm just nostalgic for my youth

Fear's not special
Fear's just romance without a private booth

Today's not special
Today's just the anniversary of defeat

Time's not special
Time just steals and then retreats

You're not special
You're just this week's entry on what I cannot live without

The only thing that I know is special
is your breath
my tears
today
our time together

And the tearful excremental magic of lusting after you that,
during momentary bouts of lucid transitory visionary trust,
evacuates all doubt

Rainbow

I do not know much about rainbows
ribbons of love
bald
translucent desire

or

two incoherent rainbows meeting in the mist of Victoria Falls
this perfect circular epiphany of light
this unitary racialized impressionistic lie
expanding nothing apart from
borders, lines,
(the televised imagined texture of his brown skin in a lime taffeta
ball gown bodice boned with tangerine sleeves)

this single circular rainbow
I do not trust
why do I always couple love
mistrust romance

or

there can be solitude and lust in the autoeroticism
of that perfect monolithic globe of insular thought and wrist
action
telling me something about
my love for myself
and masturbation
and other things

the far reaching mist of immature ejaculation
that I take great delight in whipping up, through adolescence
relived, remembered, citational bowels of
my very happy juvenalia
mild insane bacchanalian moments jerking off
just before I greet the day

circularity provides an orgiastic light
that guides me past an empty

definition of masculine loneliness
I am only alone with blank metaphors of wealth
imagined pots of gold
signifying ends

single rainbows promise everything that lies beyond their depth
but the chase is half the fun

or

when she says that
rainbows rape angels
I am startled by what I understand as
darkened metaphor
by the pale side of enlightenment
she teaches me all of this
through her agony

I am pleased
by what I do not know about rainbows
by the knowledge of the performative victim
sliding mercilessly into consciousness
mine, yours
intrusive, unapologetic, weepy, dear to me
the arch of prismatic colours formed in rain
or spray by the sun's rays

lusty lunar rainbows formed by the rays of the moon
but so dark and barely discernible to the naked body

I try to listen without asking
to ask without expectation
to take the emotional didacticism of trauma
away from myself and the people I love
with grace and fear
and the slow unchanging arch, the risk, the colour
that comes with
chasing rainbows
forever

Astound

Astound me
I believe in autumn

No, I expected summer
to last
another six months

Astound me
when summers are short

I am not disappointed in
them
I am saddened by their insensitivity

Astound me
like short men do

Seasons are never long here
nothing lasts
only winter

Astound me
I believe in autumn

it signals the end
of all that has
disappointed
me

Astound me
be unlike summer

stay, bear fruit
last forever
like some men do

Astound me

Autumn

Yes, I can believe	yes, I can believe
that fall has come	that fall has come
Promising long warm days	nights distinguishing themselves
Nights that fluctuate	the faintest chill
from the faintest chill	your almost pudding warmth
to almost pudding warmth	to this frail code
then this frail breeze	between us nothing happens
some bed of goldenrod	but the blunt insatiate
I call it ragweed	way you fuck me

promising long warm days that fluctuate the faintest chill

When you held me	mid September
mid September	these eleven months of fool's gold
You whispered, "goldenrod"	this year of snow, these
I whisper, ragweed	tools of love
instruments of love, your arms	I whisper, ragweed
could I call them	instruments of war
tools of war	could I call you

	sweetheart
villain	

yes   I   can   believe   that   fall   has   come

Invisible foreground

An old photograph
of my mother
on her boyfriend's motorcycle
his name was Mitch
She's wearing all his gear
his motorcycle drag
looking like those
vintage lesbian photographs

The stuff of which dreams
and documentaries are made
I would re-write my mother's history
if I could
But my pen is not the place
not deep enough to trace
the lines that never met
the intersections of her grief

The women she would have become
so many women my mother
could have been instead
of that nameless photograph
dressed up like Mitch
looking so comfortable
that feminine manly gaze

I store unwritten narratives
in my heart for her
my pen is never deep enough
to trace the lines

I cannot draw them for her
I cannot place my regrets
in negatives from old photographs

But I long to trade her unnamed heartache
for something more
than faded de-actualized
histories
that motorcycle
snapping that picture

Loving her butch graceful womanly body
homo-eroticizing adjectives, nouns, bodies, verbs
so close to the quick deep wet inviolable space
where I began

Spring rolls in the dead of winter

we met during intermission
I was an usher, you an
inner city schoolgirl
bussed cross town
for culture

all black musicals
Russian plays
American romantic comedies
Canadian testimonies to parodic geographic angst

talent, wanted, alive

we shared
spring rolls in the dead of winter
at Ginsberg & Wong's
gefilte fish, hot & sour
in the village
by the Grange

we were young at Dundas
I was Queen at Church

you liked the Henry Moore
I found it figuratively anal
children scrambling through jungle gym like
sphincters of playful doom

you lip synced in early March
in a tight sequined gown
to "Hey Big Spender"
in the talent competition
at the Miss Black Ontario Beauty Pageant

moved your lips and hips
as Shirley Bassey sang
a hit song from a show about
hookers with hearts of gold

I can see you now the height of nonchalance
as I cheered you on
had given you the seventy-five dollar
entrance fee

worshipped you
in my problematic whitebread iconoclastic bad boyish way
dark aureoles in the heart of spring
over racialized visualization
pornographic pomp circumstantial gape

I'm sorry

you bugged me so much
about how you thought
I wanted every man in the
bars we went to, but not you

I finally cave in
make the dream you have untrue
go out on the floor, pick up, make out
with a hot Parisian French teacher
named Luc
with an identical twin brother

he spoke so little English

"Pardon, malheureusement,
je ne parle pas Français"

it was the best relationship I have ever had

his rippled washboard stomach
like sand just after waves and just before
time can move slowly on the body
but on the beach
the defenceless sand
inhuman holiday fare
breathless wanton trans-Canadian clues
intersections, raiment, cut and colour

thank you for that fateless romance
I still fondle his name in the telephone directory, long lost love
and think of you

sorry for living up to your expectations
I have always mistaken intersections
for common ground

forgive me my daily bread

for wanting you and everyone else
in gratitude
privileged, redundant apologies, publications, journal entries,
forthcoming
my anomalous academic flair
yours
for impersonating, trespassing
transgressive showgirls

raiment, cut and colour
sequins, boas

the natives return,
Queens of the night,
for intersecting talent competitions
dark starry pageantry
celebratory dirge

show tunes for a post millennial catharsis, purge

minutes, walk-in closets, doors
white men of distinction
spend too little time on

spring rolls
in the dead of winter

enjoy the snow
Miss America

Young & Relentless

that soap oper'ish glazed retinal
azure over the shoulder fear

following open mouths
heartfelt passion

and the thought that
he may be her biological father

Karaoke monologue

Do you remember that summer in Paris
we made those karaoke videos by the river
you kept forgetting the name of the river
I kept forgetting your name
you asked me to fuck you mid-evening
on the semi-circular stone bench
built into Pont Neuf
and I kept saying that I was sorry
I had missed those months in the city of love
when Christo wrapped that bridge in gold fabric
inner city urban installation art
and you kept asking me who the hell Christo was
and accused me of being one of those people
who always drops names and places to impress others
and then we flew to Croatia, I think,
and drove along the Dalmation coast
and I didn't even bother telling you where we were
because I thought you would call me a pompous asshole
and it would have just led to some ugly argument
where I revealed to you that I had to keep
reminding the videographer
not to get any shots of you in profile
because you turn into
a very strange looking creature from the side
even though you are quite beautiful head on

(sometimes when we were fucking I had to be careful
not to let my head slip to the side over your shoulder
or I would lose my erection)

I still watch those karaoke videos
with you wandering through misty grainy avenues
of lost hope and present desire
and imagine all the housewives of varying descent
in their basements singing their hearts out
hoping to be in love like you pretended to be in those videos
if they could only see you in profile they would lose interest

it was especially hard to keep you out of profile
in the Tuilleries Gardens because it was

a long lazy strolling shot
and you kept looking to the side at the trees
and the leaves because I guess you thought
that would be what someone in love would do
but your problem

(much like my own)

was that you never really figured out what someone in love
    would do
you just followed the bouncing ball and sang along, with Mitch,
    bitch
and made indiscreet remarks about how songs like

"Torn Between Two Lovers"

really meant something special and profound to you
and I could just say that songs like

"I Don't Want to Sleep Alone"

mean a lot to me but that would be cruel
because sleeping is the only thing I don't want to do alone
the rest of the time you could have been anyone, anyone but you

you really annoyed me and we spent all that time in Turkey
after the shoot and I honestly believe
that you had no idea where you were and didn't care
and had more fun than I did just being you

maybe I have this all wrong and it was me not you or both
but I feel sometimes, honestly I do
I feel things, and people mean things to me
and I want to sing along and leave it at that but can't
and always envied and hated you a little
for being so imperfect and so happy
and then I watch that video and sing along to

"Crying Time"

or

"The End of the World"

and sometimes when I am especially whacked out I listen to

"Crazy"

and it occurs to me that this is all just way too self-reflective
and that I saw myself in you
and made you into what I could never admit to being
and would like to be sorry but am too proud to swim there
slack jawed self indulgent artist
repeat after me

self jawed slack indulgent artist

and can never admit to needing
to wanting to be up there singing
with all those people watching in armchairs
because I'm empty and you're not
and I could tell that when I saw you in profile
that limp laughing chin, those birth marks
the elongated ear lobes
and the lumps along their edges that no one but me sees

(my – opic – shallow gaze)

I always had you filmed head on because that was the only way I
could stand seeing myself

Notes at fifty

I remember my mother's meat grinder
do you remember   my rib cage in Paris
the soft pork tones   the firm pliant white and orange
of those vegetables
the way my navel sank below my hips
the sun razed dunes of my thighs and buttocks

the boiled particles of lamb   and carrot   and

      potato

the way my spell check intervenes uninvited
and takes the final e off potato and tomato for

those of

us stupid enough to forget the loss
of the dissonant vowel the alphabetic absence of so much

thought

when the definitional centres of my life
were my mother's small antiquated appliances and my

biceps and   France

are   we   ever   going   to   be   happy

I've pissed off everyone I could have had kids with
birth control comes naturally to my

temperament

when I used to get bored spanking myself over the phone
with that long term phone sex partner

I just

clapped my hands   and that seemed to satisfy him

remember me   try
sitting on that bidet at the foot of our bed on Avenue des
Gobelins
reaching new plateaus in masculine hygiene
the concave musculature
of my stomach I miss

the round white doughy strength of your massive pectorals
your wild   Errol Flynn eyes
why did you test your wings with those Irish boys and
not with me

fell backwards down those stairs drunk
your backpack broke your fall
your tale of those Irish boys broke my heart
vicarious vacuous lover   me

you always wanted to be Hemingway   without the war

          wound

imagining every café we went to in Tel Aviv
the perfect journalists' retreat
cappuccino, wine, croissants, cigarettes

I would look around and wonder how you thought
Hemingway could even fit inside one of those small cafés
you always forget how short you are

I waited in Paris for you
then ran into the metro too angry to cry   art nouveau
is so old
we were never very   young

I digress

mama's home made soup
watching the juice of all those day old gourd like brainy food
stuffs
wrangle their way through the cast iron of her ancient cog

                (the Bastille)

I remember the old washer daddy made dubious jokes about

"I never laughed so hard since the old lady got her tits caught in
the wringer"

I was always half terrified of his humour, still carry it with me like
dirty laundry

that washer
fed towels into the hard pliant mechanism and watched the
water run like so much white blood
dryers and automatics had begun to take the day
but we held back in middle class poverty
                                      that
oxymoronic state of disrepute

when house wives had no right to be women
and my adolescent legs were so beautiful
and my hair was so blonde   wrangling over
all this self invention
physical wish fulfilment
                                  is not very astute

could we meet in Paris one day
pretend we never met   chat
promise and hopeful repartee

and part
sensing passion and indifference
infectious ineffectual   physical

display

                                                           intersections
                                                           pass us by

the way the evolution of kitchen appliances, wringer washers
memory, automatic, dry, never fails

to terrify us   to save
us so much time

Remember the Xmas   (for Margaret)

your father ripped   at my chest hair
chased me round   his model train
in the   spare room

Remember the fall   I was sitting on the kitchen floor
of an illegal council flat in one of the poorest districts of London
hackneyed temporary   London lifelong housing
impermanent transient   sightseeing east ender
and you called me   from Maui

The same floor   I sat with the telephone
receiving negative results   from a walk-in clinic
three thousand miles   away

Like smelling blood   of some kind
some wild animal
gossipy male bitch

You called me   an emotional vampire
I called you honey   wrote it all down
making no sense of it   but you were there
inspiring me   remembering spring
Mrs. Stone

and loving your large   round watermelon breasts
in my face your   C   o   c   k
in my mouth   the imaginary one
we laugh   about

remembering summer   loving on the periphery of insensitivity
intolerant of husbands   margins
this search for small places   patches of chest hair

I scan the horizon   of a well lit room
from my position   on this floor

and see your father's urn   and I can laugh
and sigh   tell old tales

lie   putting Christ back into ashes   Lust

                 Ashes   Into
                 handfuls
                 handfuls   .
                 into   Dust

7 pale sonatas in praise of the French Quarter

one

1. his pectoral muscles were a dark errant symphony 2. in white hairless majesty 3. god save this aging queen 4. from the taut 5. simplistic muscle tone 6. of some prehistoric 7. phallocentric gaze

two

1. this white hairless symphony 2. caught in the majesty 3. of some 4. pre-hysteric graze 5. saves a taut well aging queen 6. from the simplistic bustle 7. of this grand digressive sub-atonal daze

three

1. your white hairless majesty 2. in banal symphonic metre 3. strays from the sub-acerbic catatonic wailing 4. of this well taught aging queen 5. who at the age of fifty-seven 6. (according to his mama) 7. is still going through a prehistoric phallocentric phase

four

1. hairless, white, taut, majestic 2. caught offshore in yachts reserved 3. for catatonic youth hystericized upon a banquet table 4. let us go then 5. through one more half deserted vowel drenched 6. grand pectoral laden prehistoric 7. masquerading maze

five

1. your white citational mornings evenings afternoons 2. hairless in the squalid dusky light 3. of prehistoric gentrifying francophonic quarters nickels dimes 4. diminished muscle tone 5. symphonic cries 6. uptown realty barns are at their definitional heart 7. a reifying racialized unedifying predictable homespun craze

six

1. to have been called a faggot by a car full of black youths 2. while sitting on the steps of a two hundred year old slave quarter in my sub-hysteric pre-cognating uptown tourist daze 3. brings history into focus 4. through some pallid over-adjectifying 5. un-subtle atonal massive muscled 6. finely sculpted cocks of Michelangelo 7. and/or the object colour that opposes the late light gold of Titian's blinding haze

seven

1. and when that last symphonic post it note is placed upon that hearth 2. that bare sub urban polar rug 3. the soft majestic verbs that plough and fold 4. the taut young nouns 5. into some massive dark white pectoral image of the way in which we separate our bodies/matters from all the othered forms of adulation 6. saving for ourselves some latent well timed pre-hysteric hairless aging 7. dark white sly syllabic praise

My poetry

lies somewhere between political critique
and the label on the back of a box of potpourri

scathing insight and room deodorizer
lavender and blue

Land

if I had known you, falling
on a cool sunny day
in early May
driving along Danforth, from Castle Frank past
our Ontarian Greece to the 401
like driving along the main street of a small town for the
rest of your life
(the DVP closed for cyclathons)
dreaming of my own cupboard
a month's supply of groceries
in part from the all-night Dominion at Mutual and Dalhousie
some 12 cans of Habitant Pea Soup from the food bank at Bay
loaves of day-old caramelized brown bread
(white bread groceterian vaudevillian denial)
If I had known you
when your rivers were wider, trees wilder
the Don was not a Parkway
the sides of the viaduct were not cross enshrined
Christianized ant traps for the limbs
of suicidal wayward souls
waters knew nothing of purification

What would I have done differently
with the knowledge of all that

land, if I had known you

Two thirds haiku on trans gender (for Tammy Wynette)

sometimes it makes me
hard to be a woman

Mother's Day (for Beth)

the big "F" fell off the Filmore Hotel
and my feminist girlfriend won a lottery
and bought the building
and changed the whole genre to
"cry in my lap" dancing
so mothers and other wayward women
could go there

and men would pay them
to let them cry in their lap
or on their shoulder
or wherever the fuck
they felt like crying
on mother's day
or any fucking
day of the week
they felt like crying
into a man's crotch
for no good reason at all

because we have all been crying into
our mother's laps
since the beginning of time
and Jocasta had to take the original rap
for it all just because she slept with our father
this misidentified reverence for Greek Tragedy
and a Hallmark greeting card and a bunch of roses
and a god damn box of chocolates
does not even begin to repair the damage

Little wild tree (sung in a delicate tremolo)

For Myrtle Marie Mesley

(CHORUS)
> *Little wild tree, little wild tree*
> *she tied plastic lemons*
> *to a little wild tree*

she squeezed the juice right out
on perch or speckled trout
then she tied those plastic lemons
to a little wild tree

yes every year come spring
when birds began to sing
she tied those plastic lemons
to a little wild tree

the birds would stop and look
as the little wild tree shook
as she tied plastic lemons to that
little wild tree

folk came from miles around
those lemons would astound
fastened to the branches of her
little wild tree

"Are they real or are they fake
on this Northern Stoney Lake
or are they simply plastic lemons
on a little wild tree"

(CHORUS)

at her cottage by the sea
her cottage by the sea
with white and yellow trimming on
her cottage by the sea

where she painted rocks and stones
the colours of her dreams
we could see the tree toads jumping
we could hear the bullfrogs scream

and how he helped her so
they made their garden grow
they sometimes used a spade
they sometimes use a hoe

at their cottage by the sea
their cottage by the sea
with white and yellow trimming on their
cottage by the sea

the poppies black and red
the sunlight on her head
as she tied plastic lemons to
a little wild tree

(CHORUS)

the wild tree grew so thin
it didn't grow too tall
it suited plastic lemons
more than any tree at all

she kept them in a bag
with tiny strands of string
and fastened them in early spring to
little wild tree

(CHORUS)

but one day they sold the sea
to wealthy bourgeoisie
who levelled, renovated
and plucked the wild tree

and then one winter's day
his loving passed away
but she went on forever
forever and one day

while boating on the sea
she saw no wild tree
and cried to know
her garden couldn't grow
nor could her wild tree

little wild tree
little wild tree
no more plastic lemons
no more lemon tree

Nana

misinformed, I imagined my grandmother as the anti-Christ
when she responded to John Lennon's death by saying
"he was just a pot-smoking hippie"
three m's the initials of her maiden name
a maid no more she proceeded to proclaim
that she never held a grudge
and always made a point of listing the grudges
she never held

"my brother Deyncourt, his nickname was Dink, sent all that
money back from the war
and Gladys kept it all"

"I always wanted my sister's house
just down the road from the corner of Armour and Parkhill
that sweet little place
with the lawn jockey painted white
but she sold it to someone else"

"she gave your father the comfort of the bottle
when she should have given him the comfort of the mind"

and then I remembered
that 666 is the sign of the devil
and three m's are more akin to
candy covered chocolate dime sized bites
and the golden arches sucking blood out of the rainforest and
surrounding environs

maybe I'm the anti-Christ
and my grandmother was just a sweet woman
who never held a grudge
and found it hard to love people that she didn't know

Sweet summer sentences

Fog has no arms
to hug the earth
no wheels to roll
but sometimes fog rolls
it hugs the earth

 I have no way
of simply loving you
without embrace and circles
little motions on your
back that roll and

Thunder has no wheels
but it rolls and
rain has no tears
but we cry there

Hiding every little felt
touch every little tear
that rolls and rolls
and pain has no…

But sometimes pain is
sweet like summer when
the warmth creates this
sentence that reminds us

Sometimes the fog hugs
the earth and sometimes
we hide in rain
sentences thunder to conceal

That pain that has
no sweet like summer
sentences that weep like
rain but rain has

No tears no feelings
hold me hug my
earth say something stupid
sometimes sweet summer sentences
embrace me

Henry Moore at Dundas and McCaul

During a conversation about Moore's piece
looking more like a vagina than an anus
and how Lipschitz told her 75-year-old sculptress friend
when she was 30
that she had to release herself sexually, to him
to become a better sculptor
she said

"heterocentricity is the bosom of the state"

and then she changed it to tits
and laughed so hard her bosom jiggled

alternate ending:

and then she changed it to tits
and laughed so hard the state jiggled

Poetry reading

I am reading a semi-fictional poem
about getting laid in Paris

during the making of a karaoke video
and the beautiful writerly woman
with the magnanimous breasts
and the blonde pectoral-less
boy poet who sometimes writes tit poems
are not looking at each other
but I can hear her and I can see him
and she is taking in knowingly
the faintly anonymous description
of my forehead, my chins, and my ear lobes

[describing these things to her friend as I read]

and he is smiling
and my own selfish perception of indiscretion
parts the lips framing the door to the roof of their mouths
and I think of the written breasts and the poetic thighs
of Adrienne Rich's floating poem
and how the beautiful calm of his young poetry belies the tumult
of her wise heaving sighs
and how adjectives verbs and nouns are only aging body parts

waiting to be defiled

stirred

and the appalling honesty of beauty
and the beautiful honesty of the appalling
and the appalling beauty of honesty
have all come together in this [in]visible moment
this configuration of four poets wanting   waiting
            to be heard

Gift for my Canadian brother

the days are cool, evenings warm
faint unhealthy drizzle by the storm porch window
barely breathing in the sordid air
apparent in the trough and low
below the lowest part of low

layers of ozone evaporating on a painted chair

we flew to Vegas for thirty-six hours
just because you seem to be my sad brother
that I love

and it really did cheer you up
and I felt better too
just seeing you smile at the slot machines
and the large breasts of the showgirls

and when you tried to play blackjack
and really didn't know what you were doing
but won four thousand dollars
and were so relieved when Celine didn't sing in French
and could not believe

(front row centre Cirque de Soleil
we re-named it circle jerque de soleil and laughed till we cried)

the small perfect muscularity of a woman's pectoral muscles
her contorted frame made you squirm
tied your penis into some kind of heavily engorged borromean knot

and I think that I have never seen a smile on your face like that
one
on your four thousand dollar face
my brother's face
since we were boys

but I am wrong in a sense
because even in your sadness you have never lost that incredulous

heart wrenching smile
of a boy perennially on the verge of excitement disappointment

and I persuaded you that it didn't really matter
that we were spending enough in a day and a half
to feed your children for a month
I'll give you money for that too

because in this dream
there is always enough

enough love
enough time
enough regret

for us to run along a North American boulevard

in an American desert at one a.m.
into the reflecting pool that shoots water in sync with Italian Opera

"if this is a replica of Lake Cuomo then I am Fred Astaire when I
fall out of bed"

the next morning we decide to take the red eye to the big apple
to visit an estranged cousin
who worked through the worst years of the AIDS epidemic
the worst years?
as opposed to the best?
in a Manhattan hospital
came home every night wondering where he was
and what he was doing there

But it is the morning after
and I'm on the floor you're on the cot
and the streets of Vegas are still bright and blistering
and waiting to take us to be taken
and the place smells like it smells

but the police officer just outside the cell says the paper work will
take some time

"jumping into the ornamental pool of a posh hotel is a serious crime"

"so much for the big apple"
you say in that low
warm
faintly unhealthy

barely breathing in the sordid air
apparent in the trough and low
below the lowest part of low
and higher still

the voice I remember seducing young women
in our little southern Ontario storey-and-a-half house late at night
and sending me downstairs to sleep on the green chintz sofa
while you took them to our boys' shared bedroom bunks
and contributed to the wonderful over-determined sexual dysphoria
that informs my every adult breath

woke me up to get you a glass of water

barely breathing in the sordid air

"But officer, we were in Italy.
I was just taking my brother on an imaginary trip
to Italy and we went for a late night swim."

And he is not amused
and I am so sure that it is a serious offence officer
so I slip him many fifties and he sneers so I slip him many more
and we are out the door!

onto the streets of Vegas
and into some simulated rickshaw

I yell and yell and yell
and laugh such an engorged full hearted heavy laugh

you give me a very strange
"did we come from the same womb!?"
kind of look
singed with such grief and abandon

and terrible terrible relief

and I give the rickshaw driver so much money
that he drags us all the way to the airport
and is so delighted with his two thousand dollar tip
that he kisses me on the shoulder

and this really is America
the America of movies that make me
very happy for a very very short time

a land of thank you's and goodbyes

that's all we need – thirty-six hours in Vegas
and an evening in New York
at a real copy of a fake Irish pub
where Guinness flows through the urinals
and it is very hard to get you out of the men's room

but here we are in heaven
ground zero
reunited with our sad rich cousin
and we are three very happy white men

cool warm
faint unhealthy storm
breathing in the sordid air
apparent and low

the lowest part of low
and higher still

and the beer and the tears are flowing like negligent reluctant smiles
when I can look at your face and try so hard to feel something about
this bond

this brotherhood of expense and emotion

"What did people do before this? It is unimaginable to me. It is
far too sad to think of."

cool days, evenings warm
faint unhealthy drizzle by the storm porch window
barely breathing in the sordid air
apparent in the trough and low
below the lowest part of low
and higher still

in this outrageous dream

                    this expansive smile

I love you

Summer on the West Nile:
a parannoyed monologue

the night the Filmore Marquee read:

"Miss Nude Toronto pageant postponed because of media hype
SARS scare
but still the best lap dancing in town"

I dreamed the big E fell out of the big SEARS sign
on the old Eaton's Centre on Yonge
and Toronto had SARS instead of SEARS

Severe *Ethnophobic* **A**cquired **R**acist **S**hopping **S**yndrome

a culture consumed by cheerless acronyms

-    **G**   ot   **A**   ids   **Y**   et   -

people wandering through Yorkville in Wonder Woman and Hello
Kitty masks
wearing socks long sleeves and pleated trousers
sweaty palms beaded with day old insect repellent
on the beach at Hanlan's Point in July

and when I'm alone in my apartment
as I prepare a screen from black mesh
and the male and female parts of stick-on velcro and staples

I fondly remember those four years in Calgary
in a basement apartment
my bicycle skidding on black ice down Home Road
on my way to my date's apartment to take him to dinner
my first clue should have been that he picked Wendy's
and all the other unmentionable clues

a list:

1 leaving his toque on while he ate

2 leaving his mittens on while he ate

3 getting relish all over his woollen fingers while he ate

4 admitting how much he loved onion rings four times
while he ate

5 never closing his mouth long enough to stop speaking and eating
at the same time while he ate

I think

there must be table manners we are all terrified of
in the same delusional way as
there must be a North American city that we are all terrified of
Calgary isn't the right size
the air pretends to be too clean
the oil fields pretend to be too mean
and all those Torontonians refusing to go to Chinatown
the size is perfect

the demographics are perfect
the likelihood of this happening at all
is perfect deflective strategy
in a city of such banal magnitude like so many cities like all North
American cities
endlessly supplying the third world with images of dull badly
dressed
people for them to dream of emulating

having moved back to Toronto when I was six
thinking believing since I was six
that every city I was in would be the one
the apocalyptic bombed city and I would be there
so I spend my life racing from town to town

trying to avoid the next catastrophic urban fall
these ice-ageist white trading centres
and now that I am forty-six – when I was forty-six
I have always had a Winnie the Pooh on the back of my toilet
surrounded by rolls of pale gold designer butt tissue

now having moved back to Toronto
Winnie still with me, flatulent little bear
she travels well
having survived strange boyfriends with bad table manners
the G8 Summit and Air Force One at the Calgary airport
and AIDS HIV and the HMV sign on Yonge Street that flashes
the future in such sour notes
prophesying musically incorrect doom
with all those pop stars littering the streets

who would have thought mosquitoes small-minded enough to have
become CIA agents
and the million dollar fountains at Dundas Square seem this
magnetic stagnant breeding ground for some new disaster

I think it's time to settle down

Information age

to have approached fifty
nearing the end of a century
of such nightmarish proportions
knowing that every hundred years
has its unspeakable tragedies
but these have been mine

lies of identity
voluptuous curves of a modern renaissance
like the afterbirth of opera
giving way to skeletal excuses for anatomy
imitations of lives

there was something sweet, acrid, unharmonious
like incense covering flatulence
like simile covering truth
in the functional fluids we exchanged happily, willingly
uncovered secrets like the depth of my love
for discovering what my penis felt like entering a body
I was not supposed to love

(the limp wristed lazy tongue
of some bitter fey
faintly macho gigolo)

to have understood passion as self-induced biopsy
of presumed sexual i.d.
who could we be, hurtling through six rooms, carports, a small
ribbed hill in back crossing just along
the brow of a creek
that I remember looking to the bottom of

as I buried goldfish at sea
named Ophelia and Porphyria
or some unnamed lady from Shalott
in tiny waxed cardboard coffins
that sank then swam

children stammering in winter wear
in front of murky screens in cybercafes
to have been given birth to
in a year of department store promise
and hegemonic ordeal

to have struggled for a knowledge of
the convoluted nature of phrasing, words, prophecy
only eleven years after the Holocaust
and not been told in those cradled years
anything of anti-semitism
save furniture stores and silk shops
merchants lining the streets of this dilapidated Venice
this newly appointed flood plain
this act of gods

anything honest of a hatred for skin colour
and the blunt erasure of other forms of sexual phantasm
has been the worst kind of this kind of barely skin deep
self-delusional conspiratorial community building
my sense of country has to offer

as a world wonderland marked by unsudden dearth
scrambling into our twenties with so much false hope
I look to provinces scarred by cities on the brink of expulsion

how do we trim our Christmas trees
and ask for thanks giving
a special complicity in joy

to have known what it could be like
to capture a clear blue image
of my twelve-year-old feet by standing shoulder deep
and staring into lake water
now diluted by civilization

as that phantom lifeguard on a shore I knew
takes on whole new meanings
with a year-round tan and a raven ponytail
beach baskets full of rock carvings crawling

spurning shelves of innovative gift shops
that speak to me in the grey flesh tones and soap stone
cold blooded impersonations my father only began
to dream of in the trenches he preferred not
to share stories of
with me as a child

I needed his tragedy
framed by an experience of war
like I needed
another hole in my head

instead I have written myself into monologic trenches
crawled through tunnels of cut rate polyester
waiting for someone to play the accordion
whenever I enter a room
wearing hand stitched bathing gear
waterproof embroidery crying – howling – out the names
of famous women I have never known

Frida, Barbra, Billie, Marilyn, Judy, Georgia, Jayne

self-identifying praxis mixing up with dark testimonial flair,
distaste
a love for country music, neo-anti-intellectualism
clear water and the millennial feeling that a thousand years
of trial and error of causes and cures
may evaporate in precipitating dew
mottling the sign on the shore at Inverlea

no swimming allowed

with the circle and the red crossbar
making its diagonal sweep
across continents waterways food chains
Pound's "Canal and Canalesque"

phrasing, words, prophecy

is it just too obvious to say that
motorboats murder placidity
and propellers mutilate the tranquil
and that many children will never learn
to swim in the same way they once did
ever again

and that even at the end of a sad bleak horizon
there is always the promise of another day
to discover that complicity of joy in

David Bateman was born and raised in Peterborough Ontario. He completed his PhD in English Literature/Creative Writing at the University of Calgary in 2002 and teaches drama, performance, and literature at various post-secondary institutions. He is also a performance artist who frequently presents new work in Canada and the U.S.